BAHAM COOKBOOK

Traditional Recipes from Bahamas

LIAM LUXE

Copyright © 2024 Liam Luxe

All rights reserved.

CONTENTS

INTRODUCTION i
APPETIZERS 1
   Conch Fritters 1
   Rock Lobster Bites 2
   Bahamian Crab Cakes 3
   Coconut Shrimp 4
   Guava Glazed Wings 5
   Bahamian Lobster Salad 6
   Seafood Salad Cups 7
   Plantain Chips with Pineapple Salsa 8
   Cassava Fries with Mango Aioli 9
   Bahamian Style Conch Ceviche 11
SOUPS AND STEWS 13
   Bahamian Fish Chowder 13
   Bahamian Chicken Souse 14
   Rock Lobster Bisque 15
   Bahamian Split Pea Soup 17
   Conch and Corn Chowder 18
   Bahamian Okra Soup 19
   Spicy Crab and Tomato Stew 20
   Bahamian Style Grouper Stew 21
   Pepper Pot Stew 23
   Bahamian Conch and Dumpling Stew 24

SALADS 26
Tropical Fruit Salad with Coconut Dressing 26

Bahama Mama Coleslaw 27

Avocado and Tomato Salad 28

Bahamian Greek Salad 29

Mango and Jicama Salad 30

Grilled Pineapple and Shrimp Salad 31

Citrus Conch Salad 32

Bahamian Black Bean Salad 33

Watermelon and Feta Salad 34

Bahamian Style Crab Salad 35

MAIN DISHES - SEAFOOD 37
Grilled Mahi-Mahi with Mango Salsa 37

Bahamian Coconut Crusted Grouper 38

Baked Snapper with Bahama Mama Sauce 40

Spicy Grilled Lobster Tails 41

Bahamian Style Crab-Stuffed Shrimp 42

Sautéed Conch with Peppers and Onions 44

Rock Lobster Thermidor 45

Bahamian Style Fish Tacos 47

Crispy Garlic Butter Shrimp 48

Bahamian Fish and Chips 50

MAIN DISHES - POULTRY AND MEAT 52
Bahamian Jerk Chicken 52

Coconut Curry Chicken 53

Bahamian Spiced Turkey 56

Pineapple Glazed Ham 57

Guava Glazed Pork Chops 59

Bahamian Style BBQ Ribs 60

Mango Chutney Chicken 62

Bahamian Fire Grilled Steak 64

Curry Goat 65

Bahamian Chicken and Rice 67

SIDE DISHES 69

Bahamian Peas and Rice 69

Baked Macaroni and Cheese - Bahamian Style 70

Fried Plantains 72

Bahamian Style Coleslaw 73

Grits and Shrimp 74

Bahamian Baked Sweet Potatoes 75

Fried Breadfruit 76

Bahamian Cornbread 77

Bahamian Style Potato Salad 78

Bahamian Johnny Cake 79

MEASUREMENT CONVERSIONS 81

INTRODUCTION

This book is all about the tasty and unique dishes that come from the beautiful islands of The Bahamas.

These recipes are meant for everyone – whether you're a cooking pro or just starting out. Whether you're making dinner for your family or having friends over, these recipes are sure to impress.

Feel free to change things up! Cooking is like an art project, and these recipes are your canvas. Add your own twist to make them perfect for you.

This cookbook is your guide to bringing a taste of The Bahamas into your home. Whether you love seafood, tropical fruits, or just trying new things, you're in for a treat.

Happy cooking!

APPETIZERS

CONCH FRITTERS

- **Servings:** 4-6
- **Time:** 30 minutes

Ingredients:

- 1 cup conch meat, finely chopped
- 1 cup all-purpose flour
- 1/2 cup bell peppers, finely diced
- 1/2 cup onion, finely diced
- 1/4 cup celery, finely diced
- 2 cloves garlic, minced
- 1 teaspoon baking powder
- 1/2 teaspoon cayenne pepper
- 1/2 teaspoon salt

- 1/4 teaspoon black pepper
- 1/2 cup milk
- Vegetable oil for frying

Instructions:

1. In a bowl, combine conch, bell peppers, onion, celery, and garlic.
2. In another bowl, whisk together flour, baking powder, cayenne pepper, salt, and black pepper.
3. Gradually add the dry mixture to the conch mixture, stirring until well combined.
4. Pour in the milk and stir until you get a thick batter.
5. Heat vegetable oil in a pan over medium heat.
6. Drop spoonfuls of the batter into the hot oil and fry until golden brown (about 2-3 minutes per side).
7. Remove fritters and place them on a paper towel to drain excess oil.

ROCK LOBSTER BITES

- **Servings:** 4-6
- **Time:** 25 minutes

Ingredients:

- 1 pound rock lobster tail, cooked and diced
- 1 cup breadcrumbs
- 1/4 cup mayonnaise
- 2 tablespoons fresh parsley, chopped
- 1 tablespoon Dijon mustard
- 1 teaspoon lemon juice
- 1/2 teaspoon Old Bay seasoning

- Salt and pepper to taste
- Cooking spray

Instructions:

1. Preheat your oven to 400°F (200°C) and lightly grease a baking sheet with cooking spray.
2. In a bowl, combine diced rock lobster, breadcrumbs, mayonnaise, parsley, Dijon mustard, lemon juice, Old Bay seasoning, salt, and pepper.
3. Mix the ingredients until well combined.
4. Scoop a tablespoon of the mixture and form it into a bite-sized ball. Repeat for the remaining mixture.
5. Place the lobster bites on the prepared baking sheet.
6. Bake in the preheated oven for 12-15 minutes or until the bites are golden brown and cooked through.
7. Remove from the oven and let them cool for a few minutes.

BAHAMIAN CRAB CAKES

- **Servings:** 4-6
- **Time:** 30 minutes

Ingredients:

- 1 pound lump crab meat, drained
- 1/2 cup breadcrumbs
- 1/4 cup mayonnaise
- 1 large egg, beaten
- 2 tablespoons fresh parsley, finely chopped
- 1 tablespoon Dijon mustard
- 1 teaspoon Worcestershire sauce

- 1/2 teaspoon Old Bay seasoning
- Salt and pepper to taste
- 2 tablespoons vegetable oil for frying

Instructions:

1. In a large bowl, gently combine crab meat, breadcrumbs, mayonnaise, beaten egg, parsley, Dijon mustard, Worcestershire sauce, Old Bay seasoning, salt, and pepper.
2. Form the mixture into small patties, about 2 inches in diameter.
3. Heat vegetable oil in a skillet over medium heat.
4. Carefully place the crab cakes in the skillet and cook until golden brown on each side, approximately 3-4 minutes per side.
5. Once cooked, transfer the crab cakes to a paper towel-lined plate to absorb excess oil.
6. Serve warm with your favorite dipping sauce or a squeeze of fresh lemon.

COCONUT SHRIMP

- **Servings:** 4-6
- **Time:** 20 minutes

Ingredients:

- 1 pound large shrimp, peeled and deveined
- 1 cup shredded coconut
- 1 cup breadcrumbs
- 1/2 cup all-purpose flour
- 2 eggs, beaten

- 1/2 teaspoon garlic powder
- 1/2 teaspoon onion powder
- Salt and pepper to taste
- Vegetable oil for frying

Instructions:

1. In a bowl, mix together shredded coconut, breadcrumbs, garlic powder, onion powder, salt, and pepper.
2. Dredge each shrimp in flour, dip into beaten eggs, and then coat with the coconut mixture.
3. Heat vegetable oil in a frying pan over medium-high heat.
4. Fry the coated shrimp for 2-3 minutes on each side or until golden brown and crispy.
5. Remove shrimp from the pan and place them on a paper towel to absorb excess oil.
6. Serve warm with a side of your favorite dipping sauce.

GUAVA GLAZED WINGS

- **Servings:** 4-6
- **Time:** 45 minutes

Ingredients:

- 2 pounds chicken wings, split at joints, tips discarded
- 1 cup guava jelly
- 1/4 cup soy sauce
- 2 tablespoons apple cider vinegar
- 2 tablespoons ketchup
- 2 cloves garlic, minced
- 1 teaspoon ginger, grated

- 1/2 teaspoon red pepper flakes (optional)
- Salt and pepper to taste
- Fresh cilantro or green onions for garnish

Instructions:

1. Preheat your oven to 400°F (200°C) and line a baking sheet with parchment paper.
2. Place the chicken wings on the prepared baking sheet, and season with salt and pepper.
3. Bake in the preheated oven for 30-35 minutes or until wings are crispy and golden brown.
4. While the wings are baking, prepare the guava glaze. In a saucepan, combine guava jelly, soy sauce, apple cider vinegar, ketchup, garlic, ginger, and red pepper flakes (if using).
5. Cook the glaze over medium heat, stirring occasionally, until it thickens slightly (about 10-15 minutes).
6. Once the wings are done baking, transfer them to a large bowl.
7. Pour the guava glaze over the wings and toss until evenly coated.
8. Garnish with fresh cilantro or green onions.

BAHAMIAN LOBSTER SALAD

- **Servings:** 4
- **Time:** 25 minutes

Ingredients:

- 1 pound cooked lobster meat, chopped
- 1/2 cup mayonnaise

- 1/4 cup celery, finely diced
- 1/4 cup red bell pepper, finely diced
- 1 tablespoon fresh parsley, chopped
- 1 tablespoon lemon juice
- Salt and pepper to taste
- Lettuce leaves for serving

Instructions:

1. In a bowl, combine chopped lobster meat, mayonnaise, celery, red bell pepper, parsley, and lemon juice.
2. Gently toss the ingredients until well mixed.
3. Season the lobster salad with salt and pepper to taste.
4. Refrigerate the salad for at least 15 minutes to allow the flavors to meld.
5. Before serving, line a serving platter or individual plates with lettuce leaves.
6. Spoon the lobster salad onto the lettuce leaves, creating an attractive presentation.

SEAFOOD SALAD CUPS

- **Servings:** 4-6
- **Time:** 20 minutes

Ingredients:

- 1/2 pound cooked shrimp, peeled and deveined
- 1/2 pound cooked crab meat, flaked
- 1/2 cup mayonnaise
- 2 tablespoons Greek yogurt
- 1 tablespoon Dijon mustard
- 1/4 cup red onion, finely chopped

- 1/4 cup celery, finely diced
- 1 tablespoon fresh dill, chopped
- Salt and pepper to taste
- Phyllo pastry cups or lettuce leaves for serving

Instructions:

1. In a bowl, combine cooked shrimp, crab meat, mayonnaise, Greek yogurt, Dijon mustard, red onion, celery, and fresh dill.
2. Gently fold the ingredients together until well combined.
3. Season the seafood salad with salt and pepper to taste.
4. If using phyllo pastry cups, fill each cup with the seafood salad. If using lettuce leaves, spoon the salad onto the leaves.
5. Arrange the filled cups or lettuce wraps on a serving platter.

PLANTAIN CHIPS WITH PINEAPPLE SALSA

- **Servings:** 4-6
- **Time:** 30 minutes

Ingredients:

Plantain Chips:

- 2 large green plantains, thinly sliced
- Vegetable oil for frying
- Salt to taste

Pineapple Salsa:

- 1 cup fresh pineapple, diced
- 1/4 cup red onion, finely chopped
- 1/4 cup cilantro, chopped
- 1 jalapeño, seeds removed and finely chopped
- 1 tablespoon lime juice
- Salt to taste

Instructions:

Plantain Chips:

1. Heat vegetable oil in a deep pan over medium heat.
2. Carefully fry the plantain slices until golden brown and crispy, about 2-3 minutes per side.
3. Remove the chips and place them on a paper towel to absorb excess oil.
4. Sprinkle with salt while still warm.

Pineapple Salsa:

1. In a bowl, combine diced pineapple, red onion, cilantro, jalapeño, lime juice, and salt.
2. Mix well until all ingredients are evenly distributed.

Assembly:

1. Arrange the plantain chips on a serving platter.
2. Spoon the pineapple salsa on top or serve it on the side.

CASSAVA FRIES WITH MANGO AIOLI

- **Servings:** 4-6
- **Time:** 40 minutes

Ingredients:

Cassava Fries:

- 2 large cassava roots, peeled and cut into fries
- Vegetable oil for frying
- Salt and pepper to taste

Mango Aioli:

- 1 ripe mango, peeled and diced
- 1/2 cup mayonnaise
- 1 clove garlic, minced
- 1 tablespoon lime juice
- Salt and pepper to taste

Instructions:

Cassava Fries:

1. Preheat the oven to 425°F (220°C).
2. In a large bowl, toss cassava fries with vegetable oil, salt, and pepper until evenly coated.
3. Spread the fries on a baking sheet in a single layer.
4. Bake for 25-30 minutes or until golden brown and crispy, turning halfway through.

Mango Aioli:

1. In a blender, combine diced mango, mayonnaise, minced garlic, lime juice, salt, and pepper.
2. Blend until smooth and creamy.

Assembly:

1. Arrange the cassava fries on a serving plate.
2. Serve the Mango Aioli on the side for dipping.

BAHAMIAN STYLE CONCH CEVICHE

- **Servings:** 4-6
- **Time:** 20 minutes

Ingredients:

- 1 pound fresh conch, cleaned and finely chopped
- 1 cup tomatoes, diced
- 1/2 cup red onion, finely chopped
- 1/2 cup bell pepper (any color), finely diced
- 1/4 cup fresh cilantro, chopped
- 1/4 cup fresh lime juice
- 2 tablespoons orange juice
- 1 jalapeño, seeds removed and finely chopped
- Salt and pepper to taste
- Tortilla chips for serving

Instructions:

1. In a large bowl, combine chopped conch, diced tomatoes, red onion, bell pepper, and cilantro.
2. Add fresh lime juice, orange juice, chopped jalapeño, salt, and pepper.
3. Gently toss the ingredients until well combined.
4. Cover the bowl and refrigerate for at least 15 minutes to allow the flavors to meld.
5. Before serving, give the ceviche a final gentle stir.
6. Serve in individual bowls with tortilla chips on the side.

SOUPS AND STEWS

BAHAMIAN FISH CHOWDER

- **Servings:** 4-6
- **Time:** 45 minutes

Ingredients:

- 1 pound white fish fillets, cut into chunks
- 1/4 cup flour
- 3 tablespoons vegetable oil
- 1 onion, finely chopped
- 2 celery stalks, diced
- 1 bell pepper, diced
- 2 cloves garlic, minced
- 1 teaspoon thyme, dried
- 1 teaspoon paprika

- 1/2 teaspoon cayenne pepper
- 4 cups fish or vegetable broth
- 1 cup coconut milk
- 2 cups potatoes, peeled and diced
- Salt and pepper to taste
- Lime wedges for serving

Instructions:

1. In a bowl, coat fish chunks with flour, shaking off excess.
2. In a large pot, heat vegetable oil over medium heat. Add the fish chunks and cook until lightly browned. Remove fish and set aside.
3. In the same pot, add onion, celery, bell pepper, and garlic. Sauté until vegetables are tender.
4. Stir in thyme, paprika, and cayenne pepper.
5. Pour in fish or vegetable broth and coconut milk, stirring well.
6. Add diced potatoes and bring the mixture to a simmer. Cook until potatoes are tender.
7. Return the cooked fish to the pot and let it simmer for an additional 5-7 minutes.
8. Season with salt and pepper to taste.
9. Serve hot with lime wedges on the side.

BAHAMIAN CHICKEN SOUSE

- **Servings:** 4-6
- **Time:** 1 hour

Ingredients:

- 1 whole chicken, cut into pieces

- 1/4 cup lime juice
- 1/4 cup orange juice
- 2 tablespoons vinegar
- 1 onion, thinly sliced
- 2 carrots, peeled and sliced
- 2 potatoes, peeled and diced
- 1 green bell pepper, chopped
- 1 Scotch bonnet pepper, seeds removed and finely chopped
- 3 cloves garlic, minced
- 1 teaspoon fresh thyme leaves
- 1 bay leaf
- Salt and pepper to taste
- Fresh cilantro or parsley for garnish

Instructions:

1. In a large pot, combine chicken pieces, lime juice, orange juice, and vinegar. Let it marinate for at least 30 minutes.
2. Add enough water to the pot to cover the chicken. Bring it to a boil, then reduce heat to simmer until the chicken is cooked through (about 30-40 minutes).
3. Remove the chicken from the pot and let it cool. Once cooled, shred the chicken into bite-sized pieces.
4. In the same pot, add sliced onion, carrots, potatoes, green bell pepper, Scotch bonnet pepper, garlic, thyme, and bay leaf.
5. Return the shredded chicken to the pot and simmer until the vegetables are tender.
6. Season with salt and pepper to taste.
7. Serve hot, garnished with fresh cilantro or parsley.

ROCK LOBSTER BISQUE

- **Servings:** 4-6
- **Time:** 1 hour

Ingredients:

- 2 pounds rock lobster tails, shells removed and meat chopped
- 2 tablespoons olive oil
- 1 onion, diced
- 2 carrots, peeled and chopped
- 2 celery stalks, chopped
- 3 cloves garlic, minced
- 1/4 cup tomato paste
- 1/4 cup all-purpose flour
- 4 cups seafood or vegetable broth
- 1 cup dry white wine
- 1 cup heavy cream
- 1 bay leaf
- 1 teaspoon dried thyme
- Salt and pepper to taste
- Fresh chives for garnish

Instructions:

1. In a large pot, heat olive oil over medium heat. Add chopped rock lobster meat and cook until lightly browned. Remove lobster meat and set aside.
2. In the same pot, add diced onion, carrots, celery, and garlic. Sauté until vegetables are softened.
3. Stir in tomato paste and cook for an additional 2 minutes.
4. Sprinkle flour over the vegetable mixture and stir to create a roux.

5. Gradually add seafood or vegetable broth, stirring constantly to avoid lumps.
6. Pour in white wine and bring the mixture to a simmer.
7. Add bay leaf, dried thyme, and the cooked rock lobster meat. Simmer for 15-20 minutes.
8. Remove the bay leaf and transfer the soup to a blender. Blend until smooth.
9. Return the blended soup to the pot and stir in heavy cream.
10. Season with salt and pepper to taste.
11. Serve hot, garnished with fresh chives.

BAHAMIAN SPLIT PEA SOUP

- **Servings:** 4-6
- **Time:** 1 hour

Ingredients:

- 1 cup yellow split peas, rinsed and drained
- 1 ham hock or smoked ham bone
- 1 onion, diced
- 2 carrots, peeled and diced
- 2 celery stalks, diced
- 3 cloves garlic, minced
- 1 bay leaf
- 1 teaspoon dried thyme
- 6 cups chicken or vegetable broth
- Salt and pepper to taste
- Fresh parsley for garnish (optional)

Instructions:

1. In a large pot, combine split peas, ham hock, diced onion, carrots, celery, garlic, bay leaf, and dried thyme.
2. Pour in the chicken or vegetable broth and bring the mixture to a boil.
3. Reduce heat to a simmer, cover the pot, and cook for about 45 minutes to 1 hour, or until the split peas are tender.
4. Remove the ham hock from the pot. Shred the meat from the ham hock and return it to the soup.
5. Remove the bay leaf and discard.
6. Using an immersion blender or transferring to a blender in batches, blend the soup until smooth.
7. Season with salt and pepper to taste.
8. Serve hot, garnished with fresh parsley if desired.

CONCH AND CORN CHOWDER

- **Servings:** 4-6
- **Time:** 45 minutes

Ingredients:

- 1 pound conch meat, cleaned and diced
- 1 cup fresh or frozen corn kernels
- 2 tablespoons olive oil
- 1 onion, diced
- 2 carrots, peeled and diced
- 2 celery stalks, diced
- 3 cloves garlic, minced
- 1 teaspoon dried thyme
- 4 cups seafood or vegetable broth
- 2 cups potatoes, peeled and diced
- 1 cup heavy cream

- Salt and pepper to taste
- Fresh chives for garnish

Instructions:

1. In a large pot, heat olive oil over medium heat. Add diced conch meat and cook until opaque. Remove conch meat and set aside.
2. In the same pot, add diced onion, carrots, celery, and garlic. Sauté until vegetables are softened.
3. Stir in dried thyme and cook for an additional 2 minutes.
4. Pour in seafood or vegetable broth, scraping any bits from the bottom of the pot.
5. Add diced potatoes and bring the mixture to a simmer. Cook until potatoes are tender.
6. Return the cooked conch meat to the pot.
7. Stir in fresh or frozen corn kernels and continue to simmer for an additional 10 minutes.
8. Pour in heavy cream, stirring to combine. Simmer for an additional 5 minutes.
9. Season with salt and pepper to taste.
10. Serve hot, garnished with fresh chives.

BAHAMIAN OKRA SOUP

- **Servings:** 4-6
- **Time:** 40 minutes

Ingredients:

- 1 pound okra, trimmed and sliced
- 1 pound chicken thighs, boneless and skinless, diced
- 1 onion, diced

- 2 carrots, peeled and diced
- 2 celery stalks, diced
- 2 cloves garlic, minced
- 1 teaspoon fresh thyme leaves
- 1 bay leaf
- 6 cups chicken broth
- 1 cup tomatoes, diced
- 1 cup corn kernels, fresh or frozen
- Salt and pepper to taste
- Hot sauce for serving (optional)

Instructions:

1. In a large pot, combine diced chicken thighs, diced onion, carrots, celery, minced garlic, fresh thyme leaves, and bay leaf.
2. Pour in chicken broth and bring the mixture to a boil.
3. Reduce heat to a simmer, cover the pot, and cook for about 20 minutes or until the chicken is cooked through.
4. Add sliced okra, diced tomatoes, and corn kernels to the pot. Simmer for an additional 10-15 minutes.
5. Season with salt and pepper to taste.
6. Remove the bay leaf and discard.
7. Serve hot, with optional hot sauce on the side for those who like an extra kick.

SPICY CRAB AND TOMATO STEW

- **Servings:** 4-6
- **Time:** 35 minutes

Ingredients:

- 1 pound crab meat, picked and cleaned
- 2 tablespoons olive oil
- 1 onion, finely chopped
- 3 cloves garlic, minced
- 1 teaspoon red pepper flakes
- 1 teaspoon paprika
- 1/2 teaspoon cayenne pepper
- 1/2 teaspoon dried oregano
- 1 can (14 ounces) diced tomatoes
- 2 cups seafood or vegetable broth
- 1 bell pepper, diced
- 1 celery stalk, diced
- Salt and pepper to taste
- Fresh cilantro for garnish

Instructions:

1. In a large pot, heat olive oil over medium heat. Add finely chopped onion and sauté until softened.
2. Add minced garlic, red pepper flakes, paprika, cayenne pepper, and dried oregano. Stir to combine.
3. Pour in diced tomatoes and seafood or vegetable broth. Bring the mixture to a simmer.
4. Add diced bell pepper and celery to the pot. Cook for 10 minutes.
5. Gently fold in the cleaned crab meat, ensuring it is evenly distributed in the stew.
6. Simmer for an additional 10-15 minutes or until the crab is heated through.
7. Season with salt and pepper to taste.
8. Serve hot, garnished with fresh cilantro.

BAHAMIAN STYLE GROUPER STEW

- **Servings:** 4-6
- **Time:** 40 minutes

Ingredients:

- 1 1/2 pounds grouper fillets, cut into chunks
- 2 tablespoons olive oil
- 1 onion, finely chopped
- 2 bell peppers (any color), diced
- 3 cloves garlic, minced
- 1 teaspoon fresh thyme leaves
- 1 teaspoon paprika
- 1/2 teaspoon cayenne pepper
- 1 can (14 ounces) diced tomatoes
- 2 cups fish or seafood broth
- 1 cup okra, trimmed and sliced
- 1 cup corn kernels, fresh or frozen
- Salt and pepper to taste
- Fresh parsley for garnish

Instructions:

1. In a large pot, heat olive oil over medium heat. Add finely chopped onion and sauté until softened.
2. Add diced bell peppers, minced garlic, fresh thyme leaves, paprika, and cayenne pepper. Stir to combine.
3. Pour in diced tomatoes and fish or seafood broth. Bring the mixture to a simmer.
4. Add grouper chunks to the pot, ensuring they are submerged in the broth. Simmer for 10 minutes.
5. Gently stir in sliced okra and corn kernels. Cook for an additional 10-15 minutes or until the grouper is cooked through and the vegetables are tender.

6. Season with salt and pepper to taste.
7. Serve hot, garnished with fresh parsley.

PEPPER POT STEW

- **Servings:** 4-6
- **Time:** 1 hour

Ingredients:

- 1 pound beef stew meat, cubed
- 2 tablespoons vegetable oil
- 1 onion, finely chopped
- 3 cloves garlic, minced
- 2 bell peppers (any color), diced
- 2 cups spinach, chopped
- 1 cup okra, trimmed and sliced
- 1 cup callaloo leaves (substitute spinach if unavailable), chopped
- 1 tablespoon cassareep (a traditional Guyanese ingredient, available in specialty stores)
- 1 teaspoon dried thyme
- 1 teaspoon ground allspice
- 4 cups beef or vegetable broth
- Salt and pepper to taste
- Cooked rice for serving

Instructions:

1. In a large pot, heat vegetable oil over medium heat. Add beef stew meat and brown on all sides. Remove the meat and set aside.

2. In the same pot, add finely chopped onion and sauté until softened.
3. Add minced garlic, diced bell peppers, chopped spinach, sliced okra, and chopped callaloo leaves. Stir until the vegetables are slightly wilted.
4. Return the browned beef to the pot.
5. Add cassareep, dried thyme, and ground allspice. Stir to coat the ingredients.
6. Pour in beef or vegetable broth, ensuring the ingredients are submerged.
7. Bring the stew to a simmer and let it cook for about 30-40 minutes or until the beef is tender and the flavors meld.
8. Season with salt and pepper to taste.
9. Serve hot over cooked rice.

BAHAMIAN CONCH AND DUMPLING STEW

- **Servings:** 4-6
- **Time:** 1 hour

Ingredients:

- 1 pound conch meat, cleaned and diced
- 2 tablespoons vegetable oil
- 1 onion, finely chopped
- 2 bell peppers (any color), diced
- 3 cloves garlic, minced
- 2 carrots, peeled and diced
- 2 celery stalks, diced
- 1 cup tomatoes, diced
- 1 teaspoon dried thyme

- 1 teaspoon paprika
- 1/2 teaspoon cayenne pepper
- 6 cups seafood or vegetable broth
- Salt and pepper to taste
- Fresh parsley for garnish

Dumplings:

- 1 cup all-purpose flour
- 1/2 teaspoon salt
- 1/2 cup water (approximately)

Instructions:

1. In a large pot, heat vegetable oil over medium heat. Add finely chopped onion and sauté until softened.
2. Add diced bell peppers, minced garlic, diced carrots, and diced celery. Sauté until the vegetables are tender.
3. Stir in diced tomatoes, dried thyme, paprika, and cayenne pepper. Cook for an additional 2-3 minutes.
4. Add diced conch meat to the pot and cook until opaque.
5. Pour in seafood or vegetable broth, ensuring all ingredients are covered. Bring the mixture to a simmer.
6. In a bowl, combine all-purpose flour and salt. Gradually add water, stirring to form a soft dough.
7. Drop spoonfuls of the dumpling dough into the simmering stew. Cover and let them cook for about 15-20 minutes or until the dumplings are cooked through.
8. Season the stew with salt and pepper to taste.
9. Serve hot, garnished with fresh parsley.

SALADS

TROPICAL FRUIT SALAD WITH COCONUT DRESSING

- **Servings:** 4-6
- **Time:** 20 minutes

Ingredients:

- 2 cups pineapple chunks
- 2 cups mango chunks
- 1 cup papaya chunks
- 1 cup kiwi slices
- 1 cup strawberries, halved
- 1/2 cup unsweetened coconut flakes

Coconut Dressing:

- 1/2 cup coconut milk
- 2 tablespoons honey
- 1 tablespoon lime juice
- 1 teaspoon vanilla extract

Instructions:

1. In a large bowl, combine pineapple chunks, mango chunks, papaya chunks, kiwi slices, and halved strawberries.
2. In a separate small bowl, whisk together coconut milk, honey, lime juice, and vanilla extract to create the dressing.
3. Pour the coconut dressing over the tropical fruit mixture and gently toss to coat evenly.
4. Sprinkle unsweetened coconut flakes on top as a final touch.

BAHAMA MAMA COLESLAW

- **Servings:** 4-6
- **Time:** 15 minutes

Ingredients:

- 1 small green cabbage, finely shredded
- 1 carrot, grated
- 1 red bell pepper, thinly sliced
- 1/2 cup pineapple chunks, diced
- 1/4 cup red onion, finely chopped

Dressing:

- 1/2 cup mayonnaise
- 2 tablespoons Dijon mustard
- 2 tablespoons honey
- 1 tablespoon apple cider vinegar
- Salt and pepper to taste

Instructions:

1. In a large bowl, combine finely shredded green cabbage, grated carrot, thinly sliced red bell pepper, diced pineapple chunks, and finely chopped red onion.
2. In a separate bowl, whisk together mayonnaise, Dijon mustard, honey, apple cider vinegar, salt, and pepper to create the dressing.
3. Pour the dressing over the coleslaw mixture and toss until the vegetables are evenly coated.
4. Refrigerate for at least 30 minutes to allow the flavors to meld.

AVOCADO AND TOMATO SALAD

- **Servings:** 4-6
- **Time:** 15 minutes

Ingredients:

- 3 ripe avocados, diced
- 2 cups cherry tomatoes, halved
- 1/4 cup red onion, finely chopped
- 1/4 cup fresh cilantro, chopped
- 1 lime, juiced
- 2 tablespoons extra-virgin olive oil
- Salt and pepper to taste

Instructions:

1. In a large bowl, combine diced avocados, halved cherry tomatoes, finely chopped red onion, and chopped fresh cilantro.
2. In a small bowl, whisk together lime juice and extra-virgin olive oil.
3. Pour the lime and olive oil mixture over the avocado and tomato mixture.
4. Gently toss the ingredients until well combined.
5. Season with salt and pepper to taste.

BAHAMIAN GREEK SALAD

- **Servings:** 4-6
- **Time:** 15 minutes

Ingredients:

- 1 cucumber, diced
- 2 cups cherry tomatoes, halved
- 1 red onion, thinly sliced
- 1 cup Kalamata olives, pitted
- 1 cup feta cheese, crumbled
- 1/4 cup fresh parsley, chopped
- 1/4 cup extra-virgin olive oil
- 2 tablespoons red wine vinegar
- 1 teaspoon dried oregano
- Salt and pepper to taste

Instructions:

1. In a large bowl, combine diced cucumber, halved cherry tomatoes, thinly sliced red onion, pitted Kalamata olives, crumbled feta cheese, and chopped fresh parsley.
2. In a small bowl, whisk together extra-virgin olive oil, red wine vinegar, dried oregano, salt, and pepper.
3. Pour the dressing over the salad ingredients.
4. Gently toss the salad until all ingredients are evenly coated with the dressing.

MANGO AND JICAMA SALAD

- **Servings:** 4-6
- **Time:** 20 minutes

Ingredients:

- 2 ripe mangoes, peeled and diced
- 1 medium jicama, peeled and julienned
- 1 red bell pepper, thinly sliced
- 1/4 cup red onion, finely chopped
- 1/4 cup fresh cilantro, chopped
- Juice of 2 limes
- 2 tablespoons honey
- 1 tablespoon chili powder (optional for a hint of spice)
- Salt to taste

Instructions:

1. In a large bowl, combine diced mangoes, julienned jicama, thinly sliced red bell pepper, finely chopped red onion, and chopped fresh cilantro.
2. In a small bowl, whisk together the lime juice, honey, and chili powder (if using).

3. Pour the dressing over the salad ingredients.
4. Gently toss the salad until all ingredients are evenly coated with the dressing.
5. Season with salt to taste.

GRILLED PINEAPPLE AND SHRIMP SALAD

- **Servings:** 4-6
- **Time:** 25 minutes

Ingredients:

- 1 pound large shrimp, peeled and deveined
- 1 pineapple, peeled, cored, and sliced
- 1 red onion, thinly sliced
- 1 red bell pepper, sliced into strips
- 1/4 cup fresh cilantro, chopped
- 1/4 cup extra-virgin olive oil
- 2 tablespoons lime juice
- 1 teaspoon honey
- Salt and pepper to taste
- Mixed salad greens for serving

Instructions:

1. Preheat the grill to medium-high heat.
2. In a bowl, toss shrimp with olive oil, salt, and pepper.
3. Grill shrimp for 2-3 minutes per side or until opaque and cooked through. Remove from the grill and set aside.
4. Place pineapple slices on the grill and grill for 2-3 minutes per side or until grill marks appear.

5. In a large bowl, combine grilled shrimp, grilled pineapple slices, thinly sliced red onion, sliced red bell pepper, and chopped fresh cilantro.
6. In a small bowl, whisk together lime juice and honey. Pour the dressing over the salad.
7. Gently toss the salad until all ingredients are coated with the dressing.
8. Serve the grilled pineapple and shrimp mixture over a bed of mixed salad greens.

CITRUS CONCH SALAD

- **Servings:** 4-6
- **Time:** 20 minutes

Ingredients:

- 1 pound conch meat, cleaned and thinly sliced
- 1 orange, peeled and segmented
- 1 grapefruit, peeled and segmented
- 1 cucumber, thinly sliced
- 1/2 red onion, thinly sliced
- 1 jalapeño, seeds removed and finely chopped
- 1/4 cup fresh cilantro, chopped
- Juice of 2 limes
- 2 tablespoons extra-virgin olive oil
- Salt and pepper to taste
- Mixed salad greens for serving

Instructions:

1. In a bowl, combine thinly sliced conch meat, orange segments, grapefruit segments, thinly sliced cucumber,

thinly sliced red onion, chopped jalapeño, and chopped fresh cilantro.
2. In a small bowl, whisk together lime juice, extra-virgin olive oil, salt, and pepper to create the dressing.
3. Pour the dressing over the conch salad mixture.
4. Gently toss the salad until all ingredients are evenly coated with the dressing.
5. Serve the citrus conch salad over a bed of mixed salad greens.

BAHAMIAN BLACK BEAN SALAD

- **Servings:** 4-6
- **Time:** 15 minutes

Ingredients:

- 2 cans (15 ounces each) black beans, drained and rinsed
- 1 cup corn kernels, fresh or frozen
- 1 red bell pepper, diced
- 1/2 red onion, finely chopped
- 1/4 cup fresh cilantro, chopped
- Juice of 2 limes
- 2 tablespoons extra-virgin olive oil
- 1 teaspoon ground cumin
- Salt and pepper to taste
- Avocado slices for garnish (optional)

Instructions:

1. In a large bowl, combine black beans, corn kernels, diced red bell pepper, finely chopped red onion, and chopped fresh cilantro.

2. In a small bowl, whisk together lime juice, extra-virgin olive oil, ground cumin, salt, and pepper to create the dressing.
3. Pour the dressing over the black bean salad mixture.
4. Gently toss the salad until all ingredients are evenly coated with the dressing.
5. Refrigerate for at least 30 minutes to allow the flavors to meld.
6. Serve chilled and garnish with avocado slices if desired.

WATERMELON AND FETA SALAD

- **Servings:** 4-6
- **Time:** 15 minutes

Ingredients:

- 4 cups watermelon, diced
- 1 cup feta cheese, crumbled
- 1/2 cup fresh mint leaves, chopped
- 1/4 cup red onion, thinly sliced
- 1/4 cup extra-virgin olive oil
- 2 tablespoons balsamic vinegar
- Salt and pepper to taste

Instructions:

1. In a large bowl, combine diced watermelon, crumbled feta cheese, chopped fresh mint leaves, and thinly sliced red onion.
2. In a small bowl, whisk together extra-virgin olive oil, balsamic vinegar, salt, and pepper to create the dressing.
3. Pour the dressing over the watermelon and feta mixture.

4. Gently toss the salad until all ingredients are evenly coated with the dressing.

BAHAMIAN STYLE CRAB SALAD

- **Servings:** 4-6
- **Time:** 20 minutes

Ingredients:

- 1 pound crab meat, picked and cleaned
- 1/2 cup red bell pepper, finely diced
- 1/2 cup celery, finely diced
- 1/4 cup red onion, finely chopped
- 1/4 cup fresh parsley, chopped
- Juice of 2 limes
- 2 tablespoons mayonnaise
- 1 teaspoon Dijon mustard
- Salt and pepper to taste
- Mixed salad greens for serving

Instructions:

1. In a bowl, combine crab meat, finely diced red bell pepper, finely diced celery, finely chopped red onion, and chopped fresh parsley.
2. In a separate small bowl, whisk together lime juice, mayonnaise, Dijon mustard, salt, and pepper to create the dressing.
3. Pour the dressing over the crab salad mixture.
4. Gently toss the salad until all ingredients are evenly coated with the dressing.

5. Serve the Bahamian Style Crab Salad over a bed of mixed salad greens.

MAIN DISHES - SEAFOOD

GRILLED MAHI-MAHI WITH MANGO SALSA

- **Servings:** 4
- **Time:** 30 minutes

Ingredients:

- 4 Mahi-Mahi fillets
- 2 tablespoons olive oil
- 1 teaspoon ground cumin
- 1 teaspoon smoked paprika
- Salt and pepper to taste

Mango Salsa:

- 2 ripe mangoes, diced
- 1/2 red onion, finely chopped
- 1 jalapeño, seeds removed and finely chopped
- 1/4 cup fresh cilantro, chopped
- Juice of 1 lime
- Salt to taste

Instructions:

1. Preheat the grill to medium-high heat.
2. In a bowl, mix olive oil, ground cumin, smoked paprika, salt, and pepper. Coat Mahi-Mahi fillets with the spice mixture.
3. Grill the Mahi-Mahi fillets for about 4-5 minutes per side or until they are cooked through and have grill marks. Cooking time may vary depending on the thickness of the fillets.
4. While the Mahi-Mahi is grilling, prepare the mango salsa. In a bowl, combine diced mangoes, finely chopped red onion, finely chopped jalapeño, chopped fresh cilantro, lime juice, and salt. Mix well.
5. Once the Mahi-Mahi is cooked, transfer the fillets to serving plates.
6. Top each fillet with a generous spoonful of mango salsa.

BAHAMIAN COCONUT CRUSTED GROUPER

- **Servings:** 4
- **Time:** 25 minutes

Ingredients:

- 4 grouper fillets
- 1 cup shredded coconut
- 1/2 cup panko breadcrumbs
- 1/4 cup all-purpose flour
- 2 eggs, beaten
- 1/4 cup coconut milk
- 1 teaspoon garlic powder
- 1 teaspoon paprika
- Salt and pepper to taste
- Vegetable oil for frying

Instructions:

1. Preheat the oven to 200°F (95°C) to keep the cooked fillets warm while preparing the batch.
2. In a shallow dish, combine shredded coconut, panko breadcrumbs, garlic powder, paprika, salt, and pepper.
3. Set up a breading station with three separate bowls: one with all-purpose flour, one with beaten eggs mixed with coconut milk, and one with the coconut and breadcrumb mixture.
4. Dredge each grouper fillet in the flour, shaking off excess.
5. Dip the fillet into the egg and coconut milk mixture, ensuring it is fully coated.
6. Press the fillet into the coconut and breadcrumb mixture, making sure it is evenly covered.
7. Heat vegetable oil in a large skillet over medium heat.
8. Fry the coconut-crusted grouper fillets for approximately 3-4 minutes per side or until golden brown and cooked through.
9. Transfer the fillets to a paper towel-lined plate to absorb any excess oil.

10. Keep the cooked fillets warm in the preheated oven while cooking the remaining batches.
11. Serve the Bahamian Coconut Crusted Grouper hot, accompanied by your favorite tropical salsa or dipping sauce.

BAKED SNAPPER WITH BAHAMA MAMA SAUCE

- **Servings:** 4
- **Time:** 30 minutes

Ingredients:

- 4 snapper fillets
- 1/4 cup olive oil
- 2 tablespoons lime juice
- 2 teaspoons garlic, minced
- 1 teaspoon dried thyme
- 1 teaspoon paprika
- Salt and pepper to taste

Bahama Mama Sauce:

- 1/2 cup pineapple juice
- 1/4 cup orange juice
- 2 tablespoons dark rum
- 1 tablespoon brown sugar
- 1 tablespoon soy sauce
- 1 teaspoon fresh ginger, grated
- 1 teaspoon cornstarch (optional, for thickening)

Instructions:

1. Preheat the oven to 375°F (190°C).
2. In a small bowl, whisk together olive oil, lime juice, minced garlic, dried thyme, paprika, salt, and pepper.
3. Place the snapper fillets in a baking dish and brush them with the prepared marinade. Let them marinate for about 15 minutes.
4. Bake the snapper fillets in the preheated oven for 15-20 minutes or until the fish is cooked through and flakes easily with a fork.
5. While the snapper is baking, prepare the Bahama Mama Sauce. In a small saucepan, combine pineapple juice, orange juice, dark rum, brown sugar, soy sauce, and grated fresh ginger.
6. Bring the sauce to a simmer over medium heat. If you prefer a thicker sauce, mix 1 teaspoon of cornstarch with a little water to create a slurry and add it to the sauce, stirring constantly until thickened.
7. Once the snapper fillets are done baking, spoon the Bahama Mama Sauce over the top.
8. Serve the Baked Snapper with Bahama Mama Sauce hot, accompanied by your favorite side dishes.

SPICY GRILLED LOBSTER TAILS

- **Servings:** 4
- **Time:** 20 minutes

Ingredients:

- 4 lobster tails, split in half
- 1/4 cup olive oil
- 2 tablespoons lime juice
- 2 teaspoons chili powder

- 1 teaspoon smoked paprika
- 1 teaspoon garlic powder
- 1 teaspoon onion powder
- 1/2 teaspoon cayenne pepper (adjust to taste)
- Salt and pepper to taste
- Fresh parsley for garnish

Instructions:

1. Preheat the grill to medium-high heat.
2. In a bowl, whisk together olive oil, lime juice, chili powder, smoked paprika, garlic powder, onion powder, cayenne pepper, salt, and pepper to create the marinade.
3. Place the lobster tails on a cutting board, and using kitchen shears, cut along the top of the shell down to the tail.
4. Brush the lobster tails generously with the prepared marinade, making sure to get the mixture between the lobster meat and the shell.
5. Place the lobster tails on the preheated grill, flesh side down. Grill for about 4-5 minutes.
6. Flip the lobster tails, shell side down, and continue grilling for an additional 4-5 minutes or until the lobster meat is opaque and cooked through.
7. Baste the lobster tails with any remaining marinade during the last few minutes of grilling.
8. Transfer the grilled lobster tails to a serving platter.
9. Garnish with fresh parsley and serve immediately.

BAHAMIAN STYLE CRAB-STUFFED SHRIMP

- **Servings:** 4
- **Time:** 35 minutes

Ingredients:

Crab Stuffing:

- 1 cup crab meat, picked and cleaned
- 1/4 cup mayonnaise
- 1 green onion, finely chopped
- 1 tablespoon fresh parsley, chopped
- 1 teaspoon Dijon mustard
- 1/2 teaspoon Old Bay seasoning
- Salt and pepper to taste

Shrimp:

- 16 large shrimp, peeled and deveined, tails intact
- 2 tablespoons olive oil
- 1 teaspoon garlic powder
- 1 teaspoon paprika
- Salt and pepper to taste

Instructions:

1. Preheat the oven to 375°F (190°C).
2. In a bowl, combine crab meat, mayonnaise, finely chopped green onion, chopped fresh parsley, Dijon mustard, Old Bay seasoning, salt, and pepper. Mix well to create the crab stuffing.
3. Butterfly each shrimp by making a deep slit along the back, cutting almost through but leaving the bottom intact.

4. Spoon a generous portion of the crab stuffing into the slit of each shrimp.
5. Place the stuffed shrimp on a baking sheet.
6. In a small bowl, mix olive oil, garlic powder, paprika, salt, and pepper. Brush this mixture over the stuffed shrimp.
7. Bake in the preheated oven for about 15-20 minutes or until the shrimp are cooked through and the stuffing is golden brown.
8. Serve the Bahamian Style Crab-Stuffed Shrimp hot, garnished with additional fresh parsley if desired.

SAUTÉED CONCH WITH PEPPERS AND ONIONS

- **Servings:** 4
- **Time:** 20 minutes

Ingredients:

- 1 pound conch meat, cleaned and thinly sliced
- 2 tablespoons olive oil
- 1 onion, thinly sliced
- 1 red bell pepper, thinly sliced
- 1 yellow bell pepper, thinly sliced
- 2 cloves garlic, minced
- 1 teaspoon fresh thyme leaves
- 1 teaspoon paprika
- 1/2 teaspoon cayenne pepper (adjust to taste)
- Salt and pepper to taste
- Lime wedges for serving

Instructions:

1. Heat olive oil in a large skillet over medium-high heat.
2. Add thinly sliced conch meat to the skillet and sauté for 2-3 minutes or until the conch becomes opaque.
3. Push the conch to one side of the skillet and add thinly sliced onion and bell peppers. Sauté for an additional 3-4 minutes or until the vegetables are tender-crisp.
4. Stir in minced garlic, fresh thyme leaves, paprika, and cayenne pepper. Sauté for another 1-2 minutes to infuse the flavors.
5. Season the mixture with salt and pepper to taste. Adjust cayenne pepper if more heat is desired.
6. Serve the Sautéed Conch with Peppers and Onions hot, accompanied by lime wedges for a burst of citrusy freshness.

ROCK LOBSTER THERMIDOR

- **Servings:** 4
- **Time:** 45 minutes

Ingredients:

Lobster:

- 4 rock lobster tails, shells split
- 2 tablespoons olive oil
- Salt and pepper to taste

Thermidor Sauce:

- 2 tablespoons unsalted butter
- 2 tablespoons all-purpose flour
- 1 cup whole milk

- 1/2 cup Gruyere cheese, grated
- 1/4 cup Parmesan cheese, grated
- 2 tablespoons Dijon mustard
- 1 tablespoon fresh lemon juice
- 1/4 cup fresh parsley, chopped
- Salt and white pepper to taste
- Pinch of nutmeg

Instructions:

1. Preheat the oven to 400°F (200°C).
2. Place rock lobster tails on a baking sheet. Brush the lobster meat with olive oil and season with salt and pepper.
3. Bake in the preheated oven for 12-15 minutes or until the lobster meat is opaque and the shells turn red.
4. While the lobster is baking, prepare the Thermidor sauce. In a saucepan over medium heat, melt unsalted butter.
5. Stir in all-purpose flour to create a roux, cooking for 1-2 minutes until lightly golden.
6. Gradually whisk in whole milk, ensuring there are no lumps. Continue stirring until the mixture thickens.
7. Reduce heat to low, and add grated Gruyere and Parmesan cheeses, Dijon mustard, fresh lemon juice, chopped fresh parsley, salt, white pepper, and a pinch of nutmeg. Stir until the cheeses are melted and the sauce is smooth.
8. Once the lobster tails are done baking, remove them from the oven.
9. Carefully spoon the Thermidor sauce over the lobster meat, ensuring an even coating.

10. Set the oven to broil and place the lobster tails back in the oven for an additional 3-5 minutes or until the sauce is bubbly and lightly browned.
11. Serve the Rock Lobster Thermidor hot, garnished with additional chopped parsley if desired.

BAHAMIAN STYLE FISH TACOS

- **Servings:** 4
- **Time:** 30 minutes

Ingredients:

Fish:

- 1 pound firm white fish fillets (such as snapper or grouper)
- 2 tablespoons olive oil
- 1 teaspoon ground cumin
- 1 teaspoon paprika
- 1 teaspoon garlic powder
- Salt and pepper to taste

Cabbage Slaw:

- 2 cups shredded green cabbage
- 1 carrot, julienned
- 1/4 cup red onion, thinly sliced
- 1/4 cup fresh cilantro, chopped
- Juice of 1 lime
- 2 tablespoons mayonnaise
- Salt and pepper to taste

Taco Assembly:

- 8 small corn or flour tortillas, warmed
- Sliced jalapeños for garnish
- Lime wedges for serving

Instructions:

1. In a bowl, combine olive oil, ground cumin, paprika, garlic powder, salt, and pepper. Brush the fish fillets with this mixture.
2. Heat a skillet or grill pan over medium-high heat. Cook the fish fillets for about 3-4 minutes per side or until they are cooked through and easily flake with a fork.
3. While the fish is cooking, prepare the cabbage slaw. In a bowl, combine shredded green cabbage, julienned carrot, thinly sliced red onion, chopped fresh cilantro, lime juice, mayonnaise, salt, and pepper. Toss until well coated.
4. Warm the tortillas in a dry skillet or microwave according to package instructions.
5. Flake the cooked fish into bite-sized pieces.
6. Assemble the tacos by placing a spoonful of the cabbage slaw on each tortilla, followed by the flaked fish.
7. Garnish with sliced jalapeños and serve with lime wedges on the side.

CRISPY GARLIC BUTTER SHRIMP

- **Servings:** 4
- **Time:** 15 minutes

Ingredients:

- 1 pound large shrimp, peeled and deveined
- Salt and black pepper to taste
- 1 cup all-purpose flour
- 2 teaspoons garlic powder
- 1 teaspoon paprika
- 1/2 teaspoon cayenne pepper (adjust to taste)
- 2 eggs, beaten
- Vegetable oil for frying

Garlic Butter Sauce:

- 1/2 cup unsalted butter
- 4 cloves garlic, minced
- 1 tablespoon fresh parsley, chopped
- Juice of 1 lemon

Instructions:

1. Season the shrimp with salt and black pepper.
2. In a shallow bowl, combine flour, garlic powder, paprika, and cayenne pepper.
3. Dip each shrimp into the beaten eggs, allowing excess to drip off, then coat them in the flour mixture, pressing gently to adhere.
4. Heat vegetable oil in a large skillet over medium-high heat.
5. Fry the coated shrimp for about 2-3 minutes per side or until they are golden brown and crispy. Work in batches to avoid overcrowding the skillet.
6. Transfer the fried shrimp to a paper towel-lined plate to drain any excess oil.

7. In a separate pan, melt unsalted butter over medium heat. Add minced garlic and sauté for 1-2 minutes until fragrant.
8. Stir in chopped fresh parsley and lemon juice to create the garlic butter sauce. Cook for an additional minute.
9. Toss the crispy shrimp in the garlic butter sauce until well coated.
10. Serve the Crispy Garlic Butter Shrimp hot, garnished with additional chopped parsley if desired.

BAHAMIAN FISH AND CHIPS

- **Servings:** 4
- **Time:** 40 minutes

Ingredients:

Fish:

- 1 pound white fish fillets (such as snapper or grouper)
- 1 cup all-purpose flour
- 1 teaspoon garlic powder
- 1 teaspoon paprika
- 1/2 teaspoon cayenne pepper
- Salt and black pepper to taste
- 1 cup buttermilk
- Vegetable oil for frying

Chips:

- 4 large potatoes, peeled and cut into thick fries
- 2 tablespoons olive oil
- 1 teaspoon garlic powder

- 1 teaspoon dried thyme
- Salt and black pepper to taste

Tartar Sauce:

- 1/2 cup mayonnaise
- 2 tablespoons sweet pickle relish
- 1 tablespoon Dijon mustard
- 1 tablespoon fresh lemon juice
- Salt and black pepper to taste

Instructions:

1. Preheat the oven to 425°F (220°C).
2. In a bowl, combine all-purpose flour, garlic powder, paprika, cayenne pepper, salt, and black pepper.
3. Dip each fish fillet into buttermilk, allowing excess to drip off, then coat them in the seasoned flour mixture.
4. Heat vegetable oil in a large skillet over medium-high heat. Fry the coated fish fillets for about 3-4 minutes per side or until they are golden brown and cooked through. Transfer to a paper towel-lined plate.
5. In a large bowl, toss potato fries with olive oil, garlic powder, dried thyme, salt, and black pepper.
6. Spread the fries in a single layer on a baking sheet and bake in the preheated oven for 25-30 minutes or until they are golden and crispy, flipping them halfway through.
7. While the fries are baking, prepare the tartar sauce. In a small bowl, combine mayonnaise, sweet pickle relish, Dijon mustard, fresh lemon juice, salt, and black pepper. Mix well.

8. Serve the Bahamian Fish and Chips hot, accompanied by a side of tartar sauce.

MAIN DISHES - POULTRY AND MEAT

BAHAMIAN JERK CHICKEN

- **Servings:** 4
- **Time:** 1 hour

Ingredients:

Jerk Marinade:

- 1/4 cup scallions, chopped
- 2 cloves garlic, minced
- 1 tablespoon fresh thyme leaves
- 1 tablespoon fresh ginger, grated
- 2 tablespoons soy sauce
- 2 tablespoons olive oil
- 1 tablespoon brown sugar

- 1 teaspoon ground allspice
- 1 teaspoon ground cinnamon
- 1 teaspoon ground nutmeg
- 1 teaspoon cayenne pepper (adjust to taste)
- Juice of 2 limes
- Salt and black pepper to taste

Chicken:

- 4 chicken leg quarters

Instructions:

1. Preheat the grill to medium-high heat.
2. In a blender or food processor, combine all jerk marinade ingredients. Blend until you have a smooth, thick paste.
3. Place chicken leg quarters in a large bowl or zip-top bag. Coat the chicken evenly with the jerk marinade, ensuring it gets under the skin and into the crevices.
4. Marinate the chicken in the refrigerator for at least 30 minutes, or preferably overnight for more intense flavor.
5. Remove the chicken from the refrigerator and let it come to room temperature.
6. Grill the chicken on the preheated grill for about 30-40 minutes, turning occasionally, until the internal temperature reaches 165°F (74°C) and the skin is crispy.
7. Allow the chicken to rest for a few minutes before serving.
8. Serve the Bahamian Jerk Chicken hot, paired with your favorite side dishes.

COCONUT CURRY CHICKEN

- **Servings:** 4
- **Time:** 45 minutes

Ingredients:

Curry Marinade:

- 1 tablespoon curry powder
- 1 teaspoon ground turmeric
- 1 teaspoon ground coriander
- 1 teaspoon ground cumin
- 1 teaspoon chili powder
- 1 teaspoon paprika
- Salt and black pepper to taste
- Juice of 1 lime

Chicken:

- 1.5 pounds boneless, skinless chicken thighs, cut into bite-sized pieces
- 2 tablespoons vegetable oil

Curry Sauce:

- 1 onion, finely chopped
- 3 cloves garlic, minced
- 1 tablespoon fresh ginger, grated
- 1 can (14 ounces) coconut milk
- 1 cup chicken broth
- 2 tablespoons tomato paste
- 1 tablespoon soy sauce
- 1 tablespoon brown sugar
- 1 lime, zest and juice
- Salt and black pepper to taste

Extras:

- Cooked white rice for serving
- Fresh cilantro, chopped, for garnish

Instructions:

1. In a bowl, combine all the ingredients for the curry marinade. Add the chicken pieces, ensuring they are well-coated. Let it marinate for at least 15 minutes.
2. In a large skillet or pot, heat vegetable oil over medium-high heat.
3. Add the marinated chicken to the skillet and cook until browned on all sides. Remove the chicken from the skillet and set aside.
4. In the same skillet, add a bit more oil if needed. Sauté chopped onions until softened.
5. Add minced garlic and grated ginger to the onions, cooking for an additional 1-2 minutes until fragrant.
6. Stir in curry powder, ground turmeric, ground coriander, ground cumin, chili powder, and paprika. Cook for another 1-2 minutes.
7. Add coconut milk, chicken broth, tomato paste, soy sauce, brown sugar, lime zest, and lime juice to the skillet. Stir well to combine.
8. Return the cooked chicken to the skillet, ensuring it's coated with the curry sauce.
9. Simmer the Coconut Curry Chicken for 20-25 minutes, allowing the flavors to meld and the chicken to cook through.
10. Season with salt and black pepper to taste.
11. Serve the Coconut Curry Chicken over cooked white rice, garnished with chopped fresh cilantro.

BAHAMIAN SPICED TURKEY

- **Servings:** 8-10
- **Time:** 3 hours

Ingredients:

Turkey Marinade:

- 1 whole turkey (12-14 pounds)
- 1/2 cup unsalted butter, melted
- 1/4 cup soy sauce
- 1/4 cup Worcestershire sauce
- 2 tablespoons fresh thyme leaves
- 2 tablespoons garlic powder
- 1 tablespoon onion powder
- 1 tablespoon paprika
- 1 tablespoon brown sugar
- 1 teaspoon ground allspice
- 1 teaspoon dried oregano
- 1 teaspoon cayenne pepper (adjust to taste)
- Salt and black pepper to taste

Stuffing:

- 2 cups breadcrumbs
- 1 cup celery, finely chopped
- 1 cup onion, finely chopped
- 1/2 cup unsalted butter
- 1 cup chicken broth
- 1 teaspoon dried sage
- Salt and black pepper to taste

Instructions:

1. Preheat the oven to 325°F (163°C).
2. Rinse the turkey under cold water and pat it dry with paper towels.
3. In a bowl, combine melted unsalted butter, soy sauce, Worcestershire sauce, fresh thyme leaves, garlic powder, onion powder, paprika, brown sugar, ground allspice, dried oregano, cayenne pepper, salt, and black pepper to create the turkey marinade.
4. Brush the turkey with the marinade, making sure to get it into all the nooks and crannies.
5. In a separate bowl, prepare the stuffing by combining breadcrumbs, chopped celery, chopped onion, melted unsalted butter, chicken broth, dried sage, salt, and black pepper.
6. Stuff the turkey cavity with the prepared stuffing.
7. Place the turkey on a rack in a roasting pan, breast side up.
8. Tent the turkey loosely with aluminum foil and roast in the preheated oven for about 2.5 to 3 hours, basting occasionally with the pan juices.
9. During the last hour of roasting, remove the foil to allow the skin to brown.
10. The turkey is done when the internal temperature reaches 165°F (74°C) in the thickest part of the thigh.
11. Let the turkey rest for 20-30 minutes before carving.

PINEAPPLE GLAZED HAM

- **Servings:** 12-14
- **Time:** 2.5 hours

Ingredients:

Ham:

- 1 fully cooked bone-in ham (8-10 pounds)
- 1 cup pineapple juice
- 1/2 cup brown sugar
- 1/4 cup Dijon mustard
- 1/4 cup whole cloves

Pineapple Glaze:

- 1 cup pineapple juice
- 1/2 cup brown sugar
- 1/4 cup Dijon mustard
- 1/4 cup honey
- 1 tablespoon cornstarch (optional, for thickening)

Instructions:

1. Preheat the oven to 325°F (163°C).
2. Place the ham in a large roasting pan, fat side up.
3. In a bowl, mix 1 cup pineapple juice, 1/2 cup brown sugar, and 1/4 cup Dijon mustard. Pour this mixture over the ham, ensuring it's well coated.
4. Score the ham by making shallow cuts in a diamond pattern. Insert whole cloves into the ham, placing them at the intersections of the cuts.
5. Tent the ham loosely with aluminum foil and bake in the preheated oven for about 1.5 to 2 hours, basting occasionally with the pan juices.
6. While the ham is baking, prepare the pineapple glaze. In a saucepan, combine 1 cup pineapple juice, 1/2 cup

brown sugar, 1/4 cup Dijon mustard, and 1/4 cup honey. Bring to a simmer over medium heat.
7. If you prefer a thicker glaze, mix 1 tablespoon of cornstarch with a little water to create a slurry. Stir the slurry into the glaze and cook until thickened.
8. During the last 30 minutes of baking, brush the ham with the pineapple glaze every 10-15 minutes.
9. Once the ham reaches an internal temperature of 140°F (60°C), remove it from the oven.
10. Allow the ham to rest for 15-20 minutes before carving.

GUAVA GLAZED PORK CHOPS

- **Servings:** 4
- **Time:** 30 minutes

Ingredients:

Pork Chops:

- 4 bone-in pork chops
- Salt and black pepper to taste
- 1 tablespoon olive oil

Guava Glaze:

- 1 cup guava juice
- 1/4 cup brown sugar
- 2 tablespoons soy sauce
- 2 tablespoons Dijon mustard
- 1 tablespoon apple cider vinegar
- 1 teaspoon garlic powder
- 1/2 teaspoon ground ginger

- 1/2 teaspoon cayenne pepper (adjust to taste)

Instructions:

1. Season pork chops with salt and black pepper.
2. In a skillet, heat olive oil over medium-high heat.
3. Sear the pork chops for 3-4 minutes on each side, or until they develop a golden brown crust. Remove from the skillet and set aside.
4. In the same skillet, combine guava juice, brown sugar, soy sauce, Dijon mustard, apple cider vinegar, garlic powder, ground ginger, and cayenne pepper. Stir well.
5. Bring the mixture to a simmer, scraping any browned bits from the bottom of the skillet.
6. Return the seared pork chops to the skillet, spooning the guava glaze over each chop.
7. Simmer for an additional 10-15 minutes, or until the pork chops are cooked through and the glaze has thickened.
8. Ensure the internal temperature of the pork chops reaches 145°F (63°C).
9. Serve the Guava Glazed Pork Chops hot, drizzled with extra glaze and accompanied by your favorite sides.

BAHAMIAN STYLE BBQ RIBS

- **Servings:** 4
- **Time:** 3 hours

Ingredients:

Ribs:

- 2 racks of baby back ribs

- Salt and black pepper to taste
- 1 tablespoon garlic powder
- 1 tablespoon onion powder
- 1 tablespoon paprika
- 1 teaspoon dried thyme
- 1 teaspoon ground allspice
- 1/2 teaspoon cayenne pepper (adjust to taste)

BBQ Sauce:

- 1 cup ketchup
- 1/2 cup brown sugar
- 1/4 cup soy sauce
- 1/4 cup apple cider vinegar
- 2 tablespoons Dijon mustard
- 2 tablespoons Worcestershire sauce
- 1 tablespoon molasses
- 1 teaspoon garlic powder
- 1 teaspoon onion powder
- 1 teaspoon smoked paprika
- 1/2 teaspoon ground allspice
- 1/2 teaspoon cayenne pepper (adjust to taste)

Instructions:

1. Preheat the oven to 300°F (150°C).
2. Remove the membrane from the back of the ribs and trim any excess fat.
3. In a bowl, mix salt, black pepper, garlic powder, onion powder, paprika, dried thyme, ground allspice, and cayenne pepper to create a rub.
4. Rub the spice mixture evenly over both sides of the ribs.

5. Place the ribs on a baking sheet lined with aluminum foil, meat side up.
6. Cover the ribs tightly with another piece of foil and bake in the preheated oven for 2.5 to 3 hours, or until the meat is tender.
7. While the ribs are baking, prepare the BBQ sauce. In a saucepan, combine ketchup, brown sugar, soy sauce, apple cider vinegar, Dijon mustard, Worcestershire sauce, molasses, garlic powder, onion powder, smoked paprika, ground allspice, and cayenne pepper. Simmer over low heat, stirring occasionally, for 15-20 minutes.
8. Once the ribs are done baking, remove them from the oven and increase the oven temperature to 400°F (200°C).
9. Brush the ribs generously with the prepared BBQ sauce.
10. Place the ribs back in the oven for an additional 15-20 minutes, or until the sauce is caramelized and sticky.
11. Allow the ribs to rest for a few minutes before slicing.
12. Serve the Bahamian Style BBQ Ribs hot, drizzled with extra BBQ sauce.

MANGO CHUTNEY CHICKEN

- **Servings:** 4
- **Time:** 40 minutes

Ingredients:

Chicken:

- 4 boneless, skinless chicken breasts
- Salt and black pepper to taste
- 1 tablespoon olive oil

Mango Chutney:

- 2 large mangoes, peeled, pitted, and diced
- 1/2 cup red onion, finely chopped
- 1/4 cup fresh cilantro, chopped
- 1/4 cup red bell pepper, finely chopped
- 2 tablespoons white vinegar
- 2 tablespoons brown sugar
- 1 tablespoon ginger, grated
- 1 teaspoon cumin
- 1/2 teaspoon cayenne pepper (adjust to taste)
- Salt to taste

Instructions:

1. Preheat the oven to 375°F (190°C).
2. Season chicken breasts with salt and black pepper.
3. In an ovenproof skillet, heat olive oil over medium-high heat.
4. Sear the chicken breasts for 2-3 minutes on each side until browned.
5. Transfer the skillet to the preheated oven and bake for about 20-25 minutes or until the chicken is cooked through.
6. While the chicken is baking, prepare the mango chutney. In a bowl, combine diced mangoes, chopped red onion, chopped cilantro, chopped red bell pepper, white vinegar, brown sugar, grated ginger, cumin, cayenne pepper, and salt. Mix well.
7. In the last 5 minutes of baking, spoon a generous amount of mango chutney over each chicken breast.
8. Return the skillet to the oven and let the chutney meld with the chicken.

9. Once the chicken reaches an internal temperature of 165°F (74°C), remove it from the oven.
10. Serve the Mango Chutney Chicken hot, spooning extra chutney over each piece.

BAHAMIAN FIRE GRILLED STEAK

- **Servings:** 4
- **Time:** 30 minutes

Ingredients:

Steak:

- 4 boneless ribeye or sirloin steaks
- Salt and black pepper to taste
- 1 tablespoon olive oil

Fire Grilled Marinade:

- 1/4 cup soy sauce
- 2 tablespoons olive oil
- 2 tablespoons Worcestershire sauce
- 2 tablespoons fresh lime juice
- 2 tablespoons brown sugar
- 1 tablespoon garlic, minced
- 1 teaspoon fresh thyme leaves
- 1 teaspoon ground allspice
- 1 teaspoon cayenne pepper (adjust to taste)

Instructions:

1. Season steaks with salt and black pepper.

2. In a bowl, combine soy sauce, olive oil, Worcestershire sauce, fresh lime juice, brown sugar, minced garlic, fresh thyme leaves, ground allspice, and cayenne pepper to create the fire-grilled marinade.
3. Place the steaks in a shallow dish or a zip-top bag and pour the marinade over them. Ensure the steaks are well-coated. Marinate for at least 15 minutes, or longer for more flavor.
4. Preheat the grill to high heat.
5. Remove the steaks from the marinade and let any excess drip off.
6. Brush the steaks with olive oil to prevent sticking on the grill.
7. Grill the steaks for about 3-5 minutes per side, or until they reach your desired level of doneness.
8. During the last minute of grilling, baste the steaks with extra marinade for added flavor.
9. Once the steaks are done, transfer them to a plate and let them rest for a few minutes.

CURRY GOAT

- **Servings:** 6
- **Time:** 2.5 hours

Ingredients:

Goat:

- 3 pounds goat meat, cut into chunks
- Salt and black pepper to taste
- 2 tablespoons curry powder
- 2 tablespoons vegetable oil

- 1 large onion, chopped
- 4 cloves garlic, minced
- 1 tablespoon fresh ginger, grated
- 2 tablespoons tomato paste
- 2 large potatoes, peeled and diced
- 4 cups water or beef broth

Curry Seasoning:

- 1 tablespoon curry powder
- 1 teaspoon ground allspice
- 1 teaspoon cayenne pepper (adjust to taste)
- 1 teaspoon dried thyme
- 1 teaspoon ground turmeric

Instructions:

1. Season the goat meat with salt, black pepper, and 2 tablespoons of curry powder.
2. In a large pot, heat vegetable oil over medium-high heat. Brown the seasoned goat meat on all sides. Remove the meat and set it aside.
3. In the same pot, add chopped onion, minced garlic, and grated ginger. Sauté until the onions are soft and translucent.
4. Stir in tomato paste and cook for an additional 2 minutes.
5. Add the browned goat meat back to the pot.
6. In a small bowl, mix 1 tablespoon curry powder, ground allspice, cayenne pepper, dried thyme, and ground turmeric to create the curry seasoning. Sprinkle this over the meat and stir to coat.
7. Add diced potatoes to the pot and pour in water or beef broth.

8. Bring the mixture to a boil, then reduce the heat to low, cover the pot, and simmer for about 2 to 2.5 hours or until the goat meat is tender.
9. Adjust seasoning with salt and cayenne pepper if needed.
10. Serve the Curry Goat hot, accompanied by rice or traditional Caribbean side dishes.

BAHAMIAN CHICKEN AND RICE

- **Servings:** 4
- **Time:** 45 minutes

Ingredients:

Chicken:

- 4 bone-in, skin-on chicken thighs
- Salt and black pepper to taste
- 1 tablespoon vegetable oil

Rice:

- 1 cup long-grain white rice
- 2 cups chicken broth
- 1 onion, finely chopped
- 1 bell pepper, diced
- 2 cloves garlic, minced
- 1 teaspoon dried thyme
- 1 teaspoon paprika
- 1/2 teaspoon ground allspice
- 1/2 teaspoon cayenne pepper (adjust to taste)
- 1 can (14 ounces) diced tomatoes, undrained

Instructions:

1. Season chicken thighs with salt and black pepper.
2. In a large skillet, heat vegetable oil over medium-high heat. Brown the chicken thighs on both sides. Remove from the skillet and set aside.
3. In the same skillet, add chopped onion, diced bell pepper, and minced garlic. Sauté until the vegetables are softened.
4. Stir in dried thyme, paprika, ground allspice, and cayenne pepper.
5. Add long-grain white rice to the skillet and cook, stirring, for 2-3 minutes until the rice is lightly toasted.
6. Pour in chicken broth and diced tomatoes with their juice. Stir well.
7. Return the browned chicken thighs to the skillet, nestling them into the rice mixture.
8. Bring the mixture to a simmer, then reduce the heat to low. Cover the skillet and simmer for 20-25 minutes or until the rice is cooked, and the chicken is cooked through.
9. Check the seasoning and adjust with salt and cayenne pepper if needed.
10. Serve the Bahamian Chicken and Rice hot, ensuring each plate has a succulent piece of chicken alongside flavorful and aromatic rice.

SIDE DISHES

BAHAMIAN PEAS AND RICE

- **Servings:** 6
- **Time:** 1 hour

Ingredients:

- 2 cups long-grain white rice
- 1 cup pigeon peas or black-eyed peas, soaked and drained
- 1 onion, finely chopped
- 1 bell pepper, diced
- 2 cloves garlic, minced
- 1 can (14 ounces) coconut milk
- 2 1/2 cups chicken broth
- 1 teaspoon dried thyme

- 1 teaspoon paprika
- 1/2 teaspoon cayenne pepper (adjust to taste)
- Salt and black pepper to taste
- 2 tablespoons vegetable oil

Instructions:

1. In a large pot, heat vegetable oil over medium-high heat. Sauté chopped onion, diced bell pepper, and minced garlic until softened.
2. Stir in dried thyme, paprika, cayenne pepper, salt, and black pepper.
3. Add soaked and drained pigeon peas or black-eyed peas to the pot, and cook for an additional 2-3 minutes.
4. Pour in coconut milk and chicken broth, stirring well.
5. Bring the mixture to a boil, then add long-grain white rice. Stir to combine.
6. Reduce the heat to low, cover the pot, and simmer for 20-25 minutes or until the rice is cooked and the liquid is absorbed.
7. Check the seasoning and adjust with salt and cayenne pepper if needed.
8. Fluff the rice with a fork, ensuring it's light and fluffy.
9. Serve the Bahamian Peas and Rice hot, as a perfect accompaniment to your favorite Bahamian main dishes.

BAKED MACARONI AND CHEESE - BAHAMIAN STYLE

- **Servings:** 8
- **Time:** 1 hour

Ingredients:

- 1 pound elbow macaroni
- 1/2 cup unsalted butter
- 1/2 cup all-purpose flour
- 4 cups milk
- 4 cups sharp cheddar cheese, shredded
- 1 cup mozzarella cheese, shredded
- 1 cup yellow onion, finely chopped
- 2 cloves garlic, minced
- 1 teaspoon mustard powder
- 1/2 teaspoon cayenne pepper (adjust to taste)
- Salt and black pepper to taste
- 1/2 cup breadcrumbs (optional, for topping)

Instructions:

1. Preheat the oven to 350°F (175°C).
2. Cook the elbow macaroni according to package instructions, then drain and set aside.
3. In a large saucepan, melt unsalted butter over medium heat. Add chopped onion and minced garlic, sautéing until softened.
4. Stir in all-purpose flour to create a roux. Cook for 2-3 minutes, ensuring the flour is well incorporated.
5. Gradually whisk in milk, making sure there are no lumps. Continue to cook and whisk until the mixture thickens.
6. Reduce heat to low and add shredded cheddar cheese, mozzarella cheese, mustard powder, cayenne pepper, salt, and black pepper. Stir until the cheeses are melted and the sauce is smooth.
7. Combine the cooked elbow macaroni with the cheese sauce, ensuring each piece is well-coated.

8. Transfer the macaroni and cheese mixture to a greased baking dish.
9. If desired, sprinkle breadcrumbs over the top for a crunchy topping.
10. Bake in the preheated oven for 25-30 minutes or until the top is golden and the edges are bubbly.
11. Allow the Baked Macaroni and Cheese to cool for a few minutes before serving.

FRIED PLANTAINS

- **Servings:** 4
- **Time:** 20 minutes

Ingredients:

- 4 ripe plantains, peeled and sliced into diagonal pieces
- Vegetable oil for frying
- Salt to taste

Instructions:

1. In a large skillet, heat vegetable oil over medium-high heat.
2. Carefully place the sliced plantains in the hot oil, ensuring they are not overcrowded.
3. Fry the plantains for 2-3 minutes on each side, or until they develop a golden brown color.
4. Using a slotted spoon, remove the fried plantains from the oil and place them on a plate lined with paper towels to absorb excess oil.
5. While still hot, sprinkle the fried plantains with salt to taste.

6. Repeat the process until all plantain slices are fried.

BAHAMIAN STYLE COLESLAW

- **Servings:** 6
- **Time:** 15 minutes

Ingredients:

Coleslaw:

- 1 small green cabbage, finely shredded
- 1 large carrot, grated
- 1 bell pepper (any color), thinly sliced
- 1/2 cup pineapple, diced
- 1/4 cup red onion, finely chopped

Dressing:

- 1/2 cup mayonnaise
- 2 tablespoons Dijon mustard
- 2 tablespoons honey
- 2 tablespoons apple cider vinegar
- Salt and black pepper to taste

Instructions:

1. In a large bowl, combine shredded cabbage, grated carrot, sliced bell pepper, diced pineapple, and finely chopped red onion.
2. In a separate bowl, whisk together mayonnaise, Dijon mustard, honey, apple cider vinegar, salt, and black pepper. Adjust the dressing to your taste.

3. Pour the dressing over the coleslaw ingredients.
4. Toss the coleslaw until all the vegetables are evenly coated with the dressing.
5. Refrigerate the Bahamian Style Coleslaw for at least 30 minutes before serving to allow the flavors to meld.
6. Before serving, give the coleslaw a final toss to ensure the dressing is well distributed.

GRITS AND SHRIMP

- **Servings:** 4
- **Time:** 30 minutes

Ingredients:

Shrimp:

- 1 pound large shrimp, peeled and deveined
- 1 tablespoon olive oil
- 3 cloves garlic, minced
- 1 teaspoon paprika
- 1/2 teaspoon cayenne pepper (adjust to taste)
- Salt and black pepper to taste
- 2 tablespoons fresh parsley, chopped (for garnish)

Grits:

- 1 cup stone-ground grits
- 4 cups water
- 1 cup whole milk
- 4 tablespoons unsalted butter
- Salt to taste

Instructions:

1. In a medium saucepan, bring water and a pinch of salt to a boil. Slowly whisk in the stone-ground grits, reduce the heat to low, and simmer. Stir frequently to prevent lumps.
2. Continue cooking the grits for 20-25 minutes, or until they are creamy and tender. Add whole milk and unsalted butter, stirring until well combined. Keep warm.
3. In a large skillet, heat olive oil over medium-high heat.
4. Add minced garlic to the skillet and sauté for 1-2 minutes until fragrant.
5. Add shrimp to the skillet, followed by paprika, cayenne pepper, salt, and black pepper. Cook for 2-3 minutes per side or until the shrimp are opaque and cooked through.
6. Spoon a generous serving of creamy grits onto each plate.
7. Top the grits with the cooked shrimp.
8. Garnish with fresh chopped parsley.

BAHAMIAN BAKED SWEET POTATOES

- **Servings:** 4
- **Time:** 1 hour

Ingredients:

- 4 medium-sized sweet potatoes
- 2 tablespoons unsalted butter, melted
- 2 tablespoons brown sugar
- 1 teaspoon ground cinnamon
- 1/2 teaspoon ground nutmeg
- Pinch of salt

Instructions:

1. Preheat the oven to 400°F (200°C).
2. Scrub the sweet potatoes thoroughly under running water to remove any dirt.
3. Place the sweet potatoes on a baking sheet lined with parchment paper.
4. Using a fork, pierce each sweet potato several times to allow steam to escape during baking.
5. Bake the sweet potatoes in the preheated oven for 45-60 minutes or until they are tender and can be easily pierced with a fork.
6. In a small bowl, mix melted unsalted butter, brown sugar, ground cinnamon, ground nutmeg, and a pinch of salt to create a glaze.
7. Once the sweet potatoes are done baking, remove them from the oven and slice each one open.
8. Drizzle the buttery glaze over each sweet potato, ensuring it seeps into the cuts.

FRIED BREADFRUIT

- **Servings:** 4
- **Time:** 30 minutes

Ingredients:

- 1 large breadfruit, peeled and cut into 1-inch cubes
- Vegetable oil for frying
- Salt to taste

Instructions:

1. Heat vegetable oil in a deep skillet or frying pan over medium-high heat.
2. Carefully add the breadfruit cubes to the hot oil, ensuring they are not overcrowded.
3. Fry the breadfruit cubes for 6-8 minutes, turning them occasionally, until they develop a golden brown color and a crispy exterior.
4. Using a slotted spoon, remove the fried breadfruit from the oil and place them on a plate lined with paper towels to absorb excess oil.
5. While still hot, sprinkle the fried breadfruit with salt to taste.
6. Repeat the process until all breadfruit cubes are fried.

BAHAMIAN CORNBREAD

- **Servings:** 8
- **Time:** 40 minutes

Ingredients:

- 1 cup cornmeal
- 1 cup all-purpose flour
- 1/4 cup sugar
- 1 tablespoon baking powder
- 1/2 teaspoon salt
- 1 cup milk
- 2 large eggs
- 1/2 cup unsalted butter, melted
- 1 cup corn kernels (fresh, frozen, or canned, drained)
- 1/4 cup diced bell pepper (any color)
- 1/4 cup diced onion

Instructions:

1. Preheat the oven to 375°F (190°C). Grease a baking dish or skillet.
2. In a large bowl, combine cornmeal, all-purpose flour, sugar, baking powder, and salt.
3. In a separate bowl, whisk together milk, eggs, and melted butter.
4. Pour the wet ingredients into the dry ingredients and stir until just combined.
5. Fold in corn kernels, diced bell pepper, and diced onion.
6. Pour the batter into the greased baking dish or skillet.
7. Bake in the preheated oven for 25-30 minutes or until the top is golden brown and a toothpick inserted into the center comes out clean.
8. Allow the Bahamian Cornbread to cool for a few minutes before slicing.

BAHAMIAN STYLE POTATO SALAD

- **Servings:** 6
- **Time:** 30 minutes

Ingredients:

- 4 large potatoes, peeled and diced
- 3 hard-boiled eggs, chopped
- 1/2 cup mayonnaise
- 2 tablespoons Dijon mustard
- 1 tablespoon apple cider vinegar
- 1/2 cup celery, finely chopped
- 1/4 cup red onion, finely chopped
- 1/4 cup green bell pepper, finely chopped

- Salt and black pepper to taste
- Paprika for garnish

Instructions:

1. Place diced potatoes in a pot of salted water. Bring to a boil and cook until the potatoes are fork-tender. Drain and let them cool.
2. In a large bowl, combine mayonnaise, Dijon mustard, and apple cider vinegar. Mix well to create the dressing.
3. Add the cooled diced potatoes to the dressing, tossing gently to coat each piece.
4. Fold in chopped hard-boiled eggs, celery, red onion, and green bell pepper.
5. Season the potato salad with salt and black pepper to taste. Adjust the seasoning if needed.
6. Refrigerate the Bahamian Style Potato Salad for at least 1 hour before serving to allow the flavors to meld.
7. Before serving, sprinkle paprika over the top for a colorful garnish.

BAHAMIAN JOHNNY CAKE

- **Servings:** 12
- **Time:** 30 minutes

Ingredients:

- 3 cups all-purpose flour
- 1 cup cornmeal
- 1/2 cup sugar
- 1 tablespoon baking powder
- 1/2 teaspoon salt

- 1/2 cup unsalted butter, melted
- 1 cup milk
- Vegetable oil for frying

Instructions:

1. In a large bowl, whisk together all-purpose flour, cornmeal, sugar, baking powder, and salt.
2. Add melted unsalted butter to the dry ingredients, mixing until crumbly.
3. Gradually pour in milk, stirring continuously until a soft dough forms.
4. On a floured surface, knead the dough briefly until it comes together.
5. Divide the dough into 12 equal portions and shape each into a ball.
6. Heat vegetable oil in a deep skillet or frying pan over medium-high heat.
7. Flatten each dough ball into a disc, about 1/2 inch thick.
8. Carefully place the Johnny Cakes into the hot oil, frying for 2-3 minutes on each side or until they turn golden brown.
9. Using a slotted spoon, remove the fried Johnny Cakes and place them on a plate lined with paper towels to absorb excess oil.

MEASUREMENT CONVERSIONS

Volume Conversions:

- 1 cup = 8 fluid ounces = 240 milliliters
- 1 tablespoon = 3 teaspoons = 15 milliliters
- 1 fluid ounce = 2 tablespoons = 30 milliliters
- 1 quart = 4 cups = 32 fluid ounces = 946 milliliters
- 1 gallon = 4 quarts = 128 fluid ounces = 3.78 liters
- 1 liter = 1,000 milliliters = 33.8 fluid ounces
- 1 milliliter = 0.034 fluid ounces = 0.002 cups

Weight Conversions:

- 1 pound = 16 ounces = 453.592 grams
- 1 ounce = 28.349 grams
- 1 gram = 0.035 ounces = 0.001 kilograms
- 1 kilogram = 1,000 grams = 35.274 ounces = 2.205 pounds

Temperature Conversions:

- To convert from Fahrenheit to Celsius: (°F - 32) / 1.8
- To convert from Celsius to Fahrenheit: (°C * 1.8) + 32

Length Conversions:

- 1 inch = 2.54 centimeters
- 1 foot = 12 inches = 30.48 centimeters
- 1 yard = 3 feet = 36 inches = 91.44 centimeters
- 1 meter = 100 centimeters = 1.094 yards.

Printed in Great Britain
by Amazon